Health and My Body

Colds

Beth Bence Reinke

a Capstone company — publishers for children

Raintree is an imprint of Capstone Global Library Limited, a company incorporated in England and Wales having its registered office at 264 Banbury Road, Oxford, OX2 7DY – Registered company number: 6695582

www.raintree.co.uk
myorders@raintree.co.uk

Hardback edition text © Capstone Global Library Limited 2022
Paperback edition text © Capstone Global Library Limited 2023
The moral rights of the proprietor have been asserted.

All rights reserved. No part of this publication may be reproduced in any form or by any means (including photocopying or storing it in any medium by electronic means and whether or not transiently or incidentally to some other use of this publication) without the written permission of the copyright owner, except in accordance with the provisions of the Copyright, Designs and Patents Act 1988 or under the terms of a licence issued by the Copyright Licensing Agency, 5th Floor, Shackleton House, 4 Battle Bridge Lane, London SE1 2HX (www.cla.co.uk). Applications for the copyright owner's written permission should be addressed to the publisher.

Edited by Gena Chester
Designed by Kazuko Collins
Original illustrations © Capstone Global Library Limited 2022
Picture research by Jo Miller
Production by Tori Abraham
Originated by Capstone Global Library Ltd

978 1 3982 2507 7 (hardback)
978 1 3982 2508 4 (paperback)

British Library Cataloguing in Publication Data
A full catalogue record for this book is available from the British Library.

Acknowledgements
We would like to thank the following for permission to reproduce photographs:
Shutterstock: A3pfamily, 12, 23, Andrey_Popov, 5, Andrii Medvednikov, 19, BlurryMe, 15, Chanintorn.v, Cover, Daisy Daisy, 27, Dawn Shearer, 9, JPC-PROD, 17, Juriah Mosin, 21, LightField Studios, 11, photonova, design element, Prostock-studio, 29, Stephanie Frey, 25, Tom Wang, 7.

Every effort has been made to contact copyright holders of material reproduced in this book. Any omissions will be rectified in subsequent printings if notice is given to the publisher.

All the internet addresses (URLs) given in this book were valid at the time of going to press. However, due to the dynamic nature of the internet, some addresses may have changed, or sites may have changed or ceased to exist since publication. While the author and publisher regret any inconvenience this may cause readers, no responsibility for any such changes can be accepted by either the author or the publisher.

Contents

What is the common cold? 4

How cold viruses spread 8

Being ill with a cold 14

Treating a cold 20

Preventing colds 24

Glossary 30

Find out more 31

Index 32

Words in **bold** are in the glossary.

What is the common cold?

Everyone gets a cold sometimes. A cold is the most common illness. That's why it is called the common cold.

A cold is an infection in the body's **airways**. Colds start in the nasal passages and throat.

A tiny germ called a **virus** causes a cold. There are more than 200 different cold viruses. Many are called **rhinoviruses**.

Anyone can get the common cold. But children get more colds than adults. Some children get up to eight colds a year.

Cold viruses are always around. You can catch a cold any time of year. But most people get colds in autumn and winter. Cold viruses spread more easily in winter. It's cold outside. People are indoors together. One person has a cold. They can spread it to others.

When people are indoors in winter, cold viruses can spread more easily.

How cold viruses spread

Cold viruses are **contagious**. This means they spread from person to person. Say a friend has a cold. You spend time with your friend at school. Soon, you get a cold too.

But how did the virus infect you? The virus is in your friend's **mucus**. It's also in **saliva**. Your friend sneezes or coughs. Droplets fly out. Droplets might hit your eyes or mouth. You might breathe in droplets too.

Droplets can spread to things people touch. Sometimes the virus gets on toys. Other children touch the toys. They touch their eyes, noses or mouths. The virus infects their bodies.

Inside the body, the cold virus gets to work. It gets inside a healthy cell. The virus takes over. The cell makes copies of the virus. Soon there are many new copies. They make the person ill.

The cold virus can be in droplets that land on toys.

When you are ill, your body fights back. Extra mucus fills your nose. Mucus in the nose traps cold viruses. Usually, mucus is clear. But it may change colour with a cold. It may turn green or yellow. That is normal. The colour is caused by helper cells.

Helper cells are made in the body. These are called white blood cells. They fight the viruses. Some helper cells eat the cold viruses. Others make **antibodies**. Antibodies fight the viruses too.

Being ill with a cold

The common cold is a mild illness. **Symptoms** start slowly. At first, your throat feels scratchy. Then you sneeze. Achoo! Your nose gets stuffy. So you breathe through your mouth. Then your throat gets sore. You might also have a low fever.

A cold can make a person cough.

A cold makes you feel tired. Your eyes can feel heavy. They might be watery too. Mucus drips down your throat. It tickles. That makes you cough. You blow your nose a lot too. That helps get rid of the mucus.

A cold lasts about a week. The cough can last a little longer. So can the sniffles.

A cold can feel like other illnesses. One illness is called the flu. The cold and the flu cause coughs and stuffy noses. But different types of viruses cause the flu.

The flu can make you feel ill faster. Plus it has other symptoms. The flu can give you a high fever. It can cause body aches too. The flu is often worse than a cold.

A thermometer can be used to check for a fever.

Treating a cold

There is no cure for a cold. But there are ways to feel better. Get a lot of rest. Go to bed early. Take naps during the day.

Fluids also help your body fight the cold. Drink lots of water. Eat ice lollies. Cool fluids soothe your sore throat. Hot drinks help too. They help loosen mucus. That helps clear your stuffy nose. Sip tea with lemon. Have some chicken soup.

Medicines can't get rid of a cold. But they might make you feel better. A trusted adult can give you medicine. Some medicines clear your nose. Others help soothe your throat.

Most people stay home while they have a cold. They take good care of themselves. But sometimes a cold lasts too long. Infections can develop. An infection can cause a high fever. It can also cause breathing problems. Then it's time to see a doctor.

Preventing colds

Vaccines help prevent the flu. People get flu jabs each year. But there is no vaccine for the common cold.

There are ways to keep from spreading a cold. Stay home when you are ill. That helps protect others. Cough and sneeze into your elbow. Use a tissue when you can. Throw it in the bin. Wash your hands straight away. Also, do not share cups or utensils.

Remember germs can get into your mouth, nose and eyes. Be mindful after you touch something in public. Don't touch your mouth or nose. Don't rub your eyes.

Wash your hands often. This helps protect you from viruses. Use warm water. Rub the soap in your palms. Scrub between your fingers. Get the tops of your hands too. Then wash your fingernails.

Wash for 20 seconds. You can set a timer. Try counting to 20 slowly. You could sing the alphabet. Hum the "Happy Birthday" song twice.

Staying healthy

Keep your body healthy to help fight cold viruses. Choose healthy foods. Eat fruit and vegetables. Drink enough water too. Get plenty of sleep. Children need 10 hours every night. Your body heals while you sleep.

Move your body every day. Your body needs exercise to stay well. Ride your bike. Play tag or go for a walk.

Relax and have fun. Laughter is good for your health. You can help yourself stay well.

Drinking water can help you stay healthy.

Glossary

airway breathing passage such as the nose, throat and lungs

antibody substance made by the body to fight germs

contagious spreads easily from person to person

mucus liquid made by cells inside the nose and breathing passages

rhinovirus type of virus that causes colds

saliva fluid that keeps the mouth moist

symptom sign the body shows when you are ill

vaccine substance that helps the body protect itself from a specific illness

virus tiny germ that can make people ill

Find out more

Books

Keeping Fit (Let's Read and Talk About), Honor Head (Franklin Watts, 2014)

See Inside Germs, Sarah Hull (Usborne, 2020)

What is a Virus?, Katie Daynes (Usborne, 2021)

Website

www.bbc.co.uk/bitesize/topics/z9yycdm/articles/zxvkd2p
Find out what the human body needs to stay healthy with BBC Bitesize.

Index

airways 4
antibodies 13

cells 10, 13
contagious 8
cures 20

doctors 22
droplets 8, 10

exercising 28

flu 18, 24
foods 28

germs 4

infections 4, 22

medicines 22
mucus 8, 13, 16, 20

relaxing 28
rhinoviruses 4

saliva 8
seasons 6
sleeping 20, 28
spreading 6, 8, 10, 24
symptoms 14, 16, 18

vaccines 24
viruses 4, 8, 10, 13, 18, 26, 28